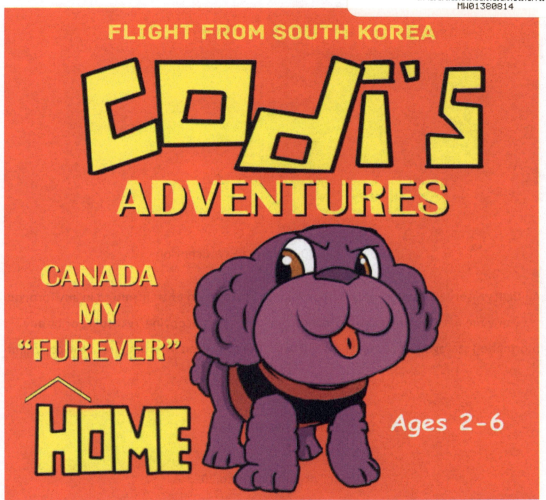

NORMA FAY NICHOLSON

Copyright @ 2023 Norma Fay Nicholson

All rights reserved. No part of this book may be reproduced or transmitted in any form or by any means, electronic or mechanical, including photocopying, recording or by any information storage and retrieval system without permission in writing from the copyright owner.

ISBN 9798860775183

Comic Format published 2023

Illustrated by Nicholas McClean

Dedication and Acknowledgment

This book is dedicated to several people who love Codi almost as much as his 'Furever' parents.

Judith Nicholson

Jane Durham

Nancy Johnson

What a wonderful day!

Judy, I think Codi is leaving South Korea soon.

They are preparing him for his flight.

Did we purchase everything he will need on his arrival?

Each time I think about owning a pet that has been

rescued, my heart leaps with joy!

Looking forward to meeting you Codi

I hope he loves his new home here in Canada.

I am going to Canada to meet my Furever family.

I am so scared.

I will grow up in Canada to become a big boy.

I am still scared because I have not been left in a crate by myself.

I am so happy that all the volunteers talked with me in our Korean language.

I hope that the other puppies will be travelling too.

I think it is because I am going to a new home.

I will play outside and have my own bed.

I will have toys and learn how to play with them.

The volunteers say that the flight takes nearly 14 hours from South Korea to Canada.

Is that a very long time to be in a plane?

I think that I will be so tired.

I will go to their home first and then travel to my Furever home.

I think we are ready to go into the plane's cargo.

We are going into the large storage space under the plane.

The windows are so small.

I hope we will be okay.

We may fall asleep during this long flight and then we won't need to be afraid anymore.

Does anyone know if you can be asleep and be afraid during sleep?

WOW!

I think we are going to fall asleep.

I am very tired too.

FLIGHT FROM SOUTH KOREA

20

Can you see me in the bubble?

This is the only window from which I can see outside when on the plane.

I am looking outside through a tiny window.

How can it be cloudy on one side of the window and sunny on the other?

We are so tired.

We are sleeping and dreaming about our new homes.

I don't know if I am dreaming but I hear a different sound than when the plane went up into the sky.

Is the plane falling from the sky now?

Are we in Canada already?

The captain says we are about to land in Toronto.

After a lengthy flight to Canada

All puppies had an opportunity to go for a walk.

Snow is falling from the sky.

It makes the ground look white, mushy, and soft.

FLIGHT FROM SOUTH KOREA

30

I overheard these two people say,

It has been snowing for a while today.

FLIGHT FROM SOUTH KOREA

I am walking in the snow.

This is different from walking on the ground.

It feels just the way it looks, mushy and soft!

I will love to play and roll in the snow.

I am alone, what happened to the other puppies?

I found them; they are eating.

I have not eaten for 14 hours.

My tummy is rumbling and making funny noises.

I joined them for a meal.

Food is good!

FLIGHT FROM SOUTH KOREA

I am so scared of needles.

I was told that all my needles were given in South Korea.

What kind of needle is this?

Why am I the first in line?

All of us puppies have now arrived safely.

Guess what?

We will travel inside a van to go to the volunteers' home.

Is this what a real home looks like?

Each bed has a different colour.

I have my own bed.

I am so happy, no more sleeping in a crate.

Oh Boy!

I am so happy.

I can run around freely.

FREEDOM!

FLIGHT FROM SOUTH KOREA

I claim this bed as my own.

It is soft and cuddly.

FLIGHT FROM SOUTH KOREA

I promptly fell asleep.

So tired from travelling for such a long time.

FLIGHT FROM SOUTH KOREA

I get to play with other puppies outdoors at the volunteers' home.

I can run as fast as I want.

I am so bitterly cold.

I thought the weather would be nice and warm here in Canada.

I see other puppies walking away without me.

I have been adopted and being driven to my Furever parents' home.

They are so happy to have me come to live with them.

I am allowed to sleep in my own bed in my parents' bedroom.

Codi Nicholson

I am starting to love my Furever family.

I have my own bed, toys, and meals served in my own dish and dessert after... this is so good.

I can run and play outside in the snow, and I do not feel very cold anymore.

I am so doggone excited it is hard to know where to begin!

I am happy that I now live in Canada.

Never returning to South Korea

Boys and Girls, please share Codi story with others.

Reflect on some of the things you learned about Codi:

1. How old was Codi when he left his first home?
2. Where was he born?
3. How many hours was his flight from his home to Canada?

4. Why do you think he wanted to return to South Korea where he had lived in a crate?
5. Where is Codi's Furever home?

FLIGHT FROM SOUTH KOREA

POTRAIT OF CODI

NORMA FAY NICHOLSON

CODI WATCHING AT THE DOOR

CODI GOES OUT ON A SNOWY DAY

CODY ON WALKING TRAIL

CODI WITH SOUTH KORIAN FRIENDS

NORMA FAY NICHOLSON

CODI WITH CANADIAN FRIENDS

CODI'S BEST FRIEND

CODI'S FAVORITE TOYS

FLIGHT FROM SOUTH KOREA

CODI'S FAVORITE FOODS

CODI'S FAVORITE BALL

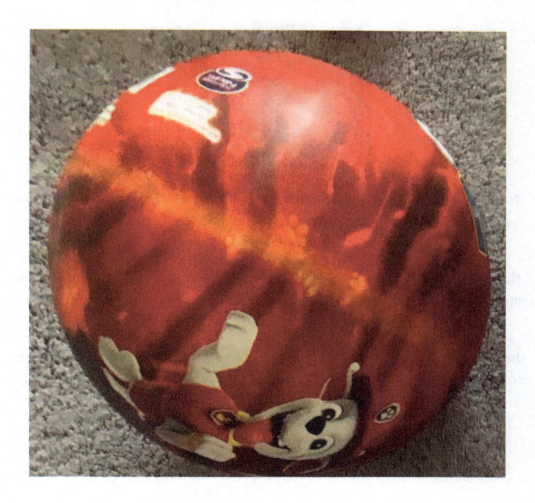

ABOUT THE AUTHOR

Norma Fay Nicholson is a retired RN with a BA and MA(Ed). She is a four-time published author, public speaker, educator, and family advocate for at-risk children and youth.

Norma has over forty years of leadership experience in a variety of healthcare sectors. She loves to volunteer to assist families in developing tools to manage the challenging behaviours of their children.

She has served on the boards of many large and impactful organizations. Due to her vibrant voice and catalyst for community growth, she has been recognized on many occasions for her advocacy and mentorship.

To order additional copies you can reach Norma Fay Nicholson at:

n.nicholson.a805@rogers.com

THE CODY BOOK SERIES

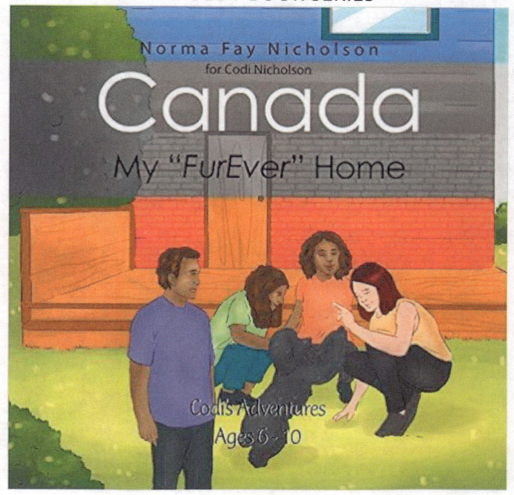

https://www.amazon.com/stores/Norma-Nicholson/author/B06Y2LSQJ8

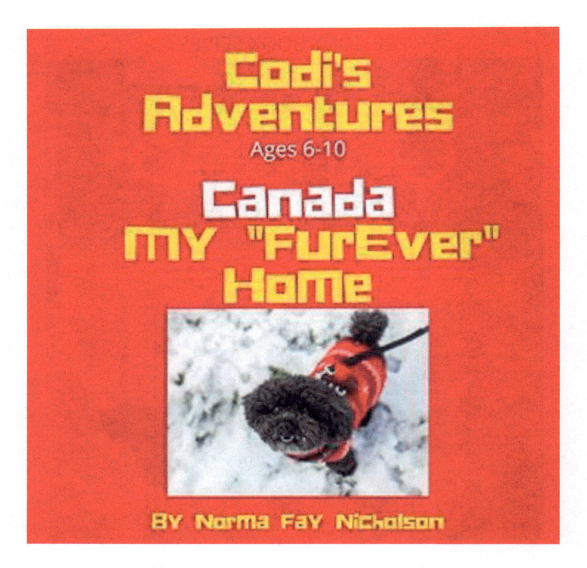

https://www.amazon.com/stores/Norma-Nicholson/author/B06Y2LSQJ8

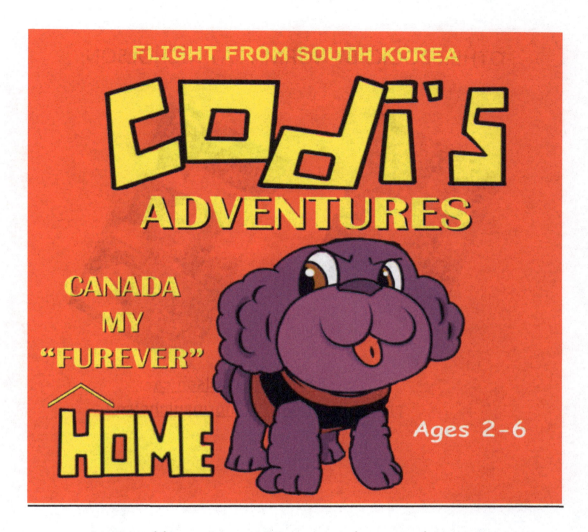

https://www.amazon.com/stores/Norma-Nicholson/author/B06Y2LSQJ8

OTHER BOOKS BY NORMA FAY NICHOLSON

www.normafnicholson.ca
amazon.com/author/normanicholson

MOM'S NOTES

FLIGHT FROM SOUTH KOREA

NORMA FAY NICHOLSON

FLIGHT FROM SOUTH KOREA

NORMA FAY NICHOLSON

FLIGHT FROM SOUTH KOREA

NORMA FAY NICHOLSON

Made in the USA
Columbia, SC
10 October 2023